Recipe Organizer for the Busy Chef
BLANK COOKBOOK

Creative Journals

Copyright © 2015 by Creative Journals

All rights reserved. This book or any portion thereof may not be reproduced without the express permission of the publisher except for the use of brief quotations in a book review.

Fine Dining at Home

Recipe #: _____

Place photo here

Ingredients:

Directions:

Fine Dining at Home

Recipe #: _____

Place photo here

Ingredients:

Directions:

Fine Dining at Home
Recipe #: _____

Place photo here

Ingredients:

Directions:

Fine Dining at Home

Recipe #: _____

Place photo here

Ingredients:

Directions:

Fine Dining at Home

Recipe #: _____

Place photo here

Ingredients:

Directions:

Fine Dining at Home

Recipe #: _____

Place photo here

Ingredients:

Directions:

Fine Dining at Home

Recipe #: _____

Place photo here

Ingredients:

Directions:

Fine Dining at Home

Recipe #: _____

Place photo here

Ingredients:

Directions:

Fine Dining at Home

Recipe #: _____

Place photo here

Ingredients:

Directions:

Fine Dining at Home

Recipe #: _____

Place photo here

Ingredients:

Directions:

Fine Dining at Home

Recipe #: _____

Place photo here

Ingredients:

Directions:

Fine Dining at Home

Recipe #: _____

Place photo here

Ingredients:

Directions:

Fine Dining at Home

Recipe #: _____

Place photo here

Ingredients:

Directions:

Fine Dining at Home

Recipe #: _____

Place photo here

Ingredients:

Directions:

Fine Dining at Home
Recipe #: _____

Place photo here

Ingredients:

Directions:

Fine Dining at Home

Recipe #: _____

Place photo here

Ingredients:

Directions:

Fine Dining at Home

Recipe #: _____

Place photo here

Ingredients:

Directions:

Fine Dining at Home

Recipe #: _____

Place photo here

Ingredients:

Directions:

Fine Dining at Home
Recipe #: _____

Place photo here

Ingredients:

Directions:

Fine Dining at Home

Recipe #: _____

Place photo here

Ingredients:

Directions:

Fine Dining at Home

Recipe #: _____

Place photo here

Ingredients:

Directions:

Fine Dining at Home

Recipe #: _____

Place photo here

Ingredients:

Directions:

Fine Dining at Home

Recipe #: _____

Place photo here

Ingredients:

Directions:

Fine Dining at Home

Recipe #: _____

Place photo here

Ingredients:

Directions:

Fine Dining at Home

Recipe #: _____

Place photo here

Ingredients:

Directions:

Fine Dining at Home

Recipe #: _____

Place photo here

Ingredients:

Directions:

Fine Dining at Home

Recipe #: _____

Place photo here

Ingredients:

Directions:

Fine Dining at Home

Recipe #: _____

Place photo here

Ingredients:

Directions:

Fine Dining at Home

Recipe #: _____

Place photo here

Ingredients:

Directions:

Fine Dining at Home

Recipe #: _____

Place photo here

Ingredients:

Directions:

Fine Dining at Home

Recipe #: _____

Place photo here

Ingredients:

Directions:

Fine Dining at Home

Recipe #: _____

Place photo here

Ingredients:

Directions:

Fine Dining at Home

Recipe #: _____

Place photo here

Ingredients:

Directions:

Fine Dining at Home

Recipe #: _____

Place photo here

Ingredients:

Directions:

Fine Dining at Home

Recipe #: _____

Place photo here

Ingredients:

Directions:

Fine Dining at Home

Recipe #: _____

Place photo here

Ingredients:

Directions:

Fine Dining at Home

Recipe #: _____

Place photo here

Ingredients:

Directions:

Fine Dining at Home

Recipe #: _____

Place photo here

Ingredients:

Directions:

Fine Dining at Home

Recipe #: _____

Place photo here

Ingredients:

Directions:

Fine Dining at Home

Recipe #: _____

Place photo here

Ingredients:

Directions:

Fine Dining at Home

Recipe #: _____

Place photo here

Ingredients:

Directions:

Fine Dining at Home

Recipe #: _____

Place photo here

Ingredients:

Directions:

Fine Dining at Home

Recipe #: _____

Place photo here

Ingredients:

Directions:

Fine Dining at Home

Recipe #: _____

Place photo here

Ingredients:

Directions:

Fine Dining at Home

Recipe #: _____

Place photo here

Ingredients:

Directions:

Fine Dining at Home

Recipe #: _____

Place photo here

Ingredients:

Directions:

Fine Dining at Home

Recipe #: _____

Place photo here

Ingredients:

Directions:

Fine Dining at Home

Recipe #: _____

Place photo here

Ingredients:

Directions:

Fine Dining at Home

Recipe #: _____

Place photo here

Ingredients:

Directions:

Fine Dining at Home

Recipe #: _____

Place photo here

Ingredients:

Directions:

Fine Dining at Home

Recipe #: _____

Place photo here

Ingredients:

Directions:

Fine Dining at Home
Recipe #: _____

Place photo here

Ingredients:

Directions:

Fine Dining at Home

Recipe #: _____

Place photo here

Ingredients:

Directions:

Fine Dining at Home

Recipe #: _____

Place photo here

Ingredients:

Directions:

Fine Dining at Home

Recipe #: _____

Place photo here

Ingredients:

Directions:

Fine Dining at Home

Recipe #: _____

Place photo here

Ingredients:

Directions:

Fine Dining at Home

Recipe #: _____

Place photo here

Ingredients:

Directions:

Fine Dining at Home
Recipe #: _____

Place photo here

Ingredients:

Directions:

Fine Dining at Home

Recipe #: _____

Place photo here

Ingredients:

Directions:

Fine Dining at Home

Recipe #: _____

Place photo here

Ingredients:

Directions:

Fine Dining at Home

Recipe #: _____

Place photo here

Ingredients:

Directions:

Fine Dining at Home

Recipe #: _____

Place photo here

Ingredients:

Directions:

Fine Dining at Home
Recipe #: _____

Place photo here

Ingredients:

Directions:

Fine Dining at Home

Recipe #: _____

Place photo here

Ingredients:

Directions:

Fine Dining at Home

Recipe #: _____

Place photo here

Ingredients:

Directions:

Fine Dining at Home

Recipe #: _____

Place photo here

Ingredients:

Directions:

Fine Dining at Home

Recipe #: _____

Place photo here

Ingredients:

Directions:

Fine Dining at Home

Recipe #: _____

Place photo here

Ingredients:

Directions:

Fine Dining at Home

Recipe #: _____

Place photo here

Ingredients:

Directions:

Fine Dining at Home

Recipe #: _____

Place photo here

Ingredients:

Directions:

Fine Dining at Home

Recipe #: _____

Place photo here

Ingredients:

Directions:

Fine Dining at Home

Recipe #: _____

Place photo here

Ingredients:

Directions:

Fine Dining at Home

Recipe #: _____

Place photo here

Ingredients:

Directions:

Fine Dining at Home

Recipe #: _____

Place photo here

Ingredients:

Directions:

Fine Dining at Home

Recipe #: _____

Place photo here

Ingredients:

Directions:

Fine Dining at Home

Recipe #: _____

Place photo here

Ingredients:

Directions:

Fine Dining at Home

Recipe #: _____

Place photo here

Ingredients:

Directions:

Fine Dining at Home

Recipe #: _____

Place photo here

Ingredients:

Directions:

Fine Dining at Home

Recipe #: _____

Place photo here

Ingredients:

Directions:

Fine Dining at Home

Recipe #: _____

Place photo here

Ingredients:

Directions:

Fine Dining at Home

Recipe #: _____

Place photo here

Ingredients:

Directions:

Fine Dining at Home

Recipe #: _____

Place photo here

Ingredients:

Directions:

Fine Dining at Home

Recipe #: _____

Place photo here

Ingredients:

Directions:

Fine Dining at Home

Recipe #: _____

Place photo here

Ingredients:

Directions:

Fine Dining at Home

Recipe #: _____

Place photo here

Ingredients:

Directions:

Fine Dining at Home

Recipe #: _____

Place photo here

Ingredients:

Directions:

Fine Dining at Home

Recipe #: _____

Place photo here

Ingredients:

Directions:

Fine Dining at Home

Recipe #: _____

Place photo here

Ingredients:

Directions:

Fine Dining at Home

Recipe #: _____

Place photo here

Ingredients:

Directions:

Fine Dining at Home

Recipe #: _____

Place photo here

Ingredients:

Directions:

Fine Dining at Home

Recipe #: _____

Place photo here

Ingredients:

Directions:

Fine Dining at Home

Recipe #: _____

Place photo here

Ingredients:

Directions:

Fine Dining at Home

Recipe #: _____

Place photo here

Ingredients:

Directions:

Fine Dining at Home

Recipe #: _____

Place photo here

Ingredients:

Directions:

Fine Dining at Home

Recipe #: _____

Place photo here

Ingredients:

Directions:

Fine Dining at Home

Recipe #: _____

Place photo here

Ingredients:

Directions:

Fine Dining at Home

Recipe #: _____

Place photo here

Ingredients:

Directions:

Fine Dining at Home

Recipe #: _____

Place photo here

Ingredients:

Directions:

Fine Dining at Home

Recipe #: _____

Place photo here

Ingredients:

Directions:

Fine Dining at Home

Recipe #: _____

Place photo here

Ingredients:

Directions:

Fine Dining at Home

Recipe #: _____

Place photo here

Ingredients:

Directions:

Fine Dining at Home

Recipe #: _____

Place photo here

Ingredients:

Directions:

Fine Dining at Home

Recipe #: _____

Place photo here

Ingredients:

Directions:

Fine Dining at Home

Recipe #: _____

Place photo here

Ingredients:

Directions:

Fine Dining at Home

Recipe #: _____

Place photo here

Ingredients:

Directions:

Fine Dining at Home

Recipe #: _____

Place photo here

Ingredients:

Directions:

Fine Dining at Home

Recipe #: _____

Place photo here

Ingredients:

Directions:

Fine Dining at Home

Recipe #: _____

Place photo here

Ingredients:

Directions:

Fine Dining at Home

Recipe #: _____

Place photo here

Ingredients:

Directions:

Fine Dining at Home

Recipe #: _____

Place photo here

Ingredients:

Directions:

Fine Dining at Home

Recipe #: _____

Place photo here

Ingredients:

Directions:

Fine Dining at Home

Recipe #: _____

Place photo here

Ingredients:

Directions:

Fine Dining at Home

Recipe #: _____

Place photo here

Ingredients:

Directions:

Fine Dining at Home

Recipe #: _____

Place photo here

Ingredients:

Directions:

Fine Dining at Home
Recipe #: _____

Place photo here

Ingredients:

Directions:

Fine Dining at Home

Recipe #: _____

Place photo here

Ingredients:

Directions:

Fine Dining at Home

Recipe #: _____

Place photo here

Ingredients:

Directions:

Fine Dining at Home

Recipe #: _____

Place photo here

Ingredients:

Directions:

Fine Dining at Home

Recipe #: _____

Place photo here

Ingredients:

Directions:

Fine Dining at Home

Recipe #: _____

Place photo here

Ingredients:

Directions:

Fine Dining at Home

Recipe #: _____

Place photo here

Ingredients:

Directions:

Fine Dining at Home

Recipe #: _____

Place photo here

Ingredients:

Directions:

Fine Dining at Home

Recipe #: _____

Place photo here

Ingredients:

Directions:

Fine Dining at Home

Recipe #: _____

Place photo here

Ingredients:

Directions:

Fine Dining at Home

Recipe #: _____

Place photo here

Ingredients:

Directions:

Fine Dining at Home

Recipe #: _____

Place photo here

Ingredients:

Directions:

Fine Dining at Home

Recipe #: _____

Place photo here

Ingredients:

Directions:

Fine Dining at Home

Recipe #: _____

Place photo here

Ingredients:

Directions:

Fine Dining at Home

Recipe #: _____

Place photo here

Ingredients:

Directions:

Fine Dining at Home

Recipe #: _____

Place photo here

Ingredients:

Directions:

Fine Dining at Home

Recipe #: _____

Place photo here

Ingredients:

Directions:

Fine Dining at Home

Recipe #: _____

Place photo here

Ingredients:

Directions:

Fine Dining at Home

Recipe #: _____

Place photo here

Ingredients:

Directions:

Fine Dining at Home

Recipe #: _____

Place photo here

Ingredients:

Directions:

Fine Dining at Home

Recipe #: _____

Place photo here

Ingredients:

Directions:

Fine Dining at Home

Recipe #: _____

Place photo here

Ingredients:

Directions:

Fine Dining at Home

Recipe #: _____

Place photo here

Ingredients:

Directions:

Fine Dining at Home

Recipe #: _____

Place photo here

Ingredients:

Directions:

Fine Dining at Home
Recipe #: _____

Place photo here

Ingredients:

Directions:

Fine Dining at Home
Recipe #: _____

Place photo here

Ingredients:

Directions:

Fine Dining at Home

Recipe #: _____

Place photo here

Ingredients:

Directions:

Fine Dining at Home

Recipe #: _____

Place photo here

Ingredients:

Directions:

Fine Dining at Home

Recipe #: _____

Place photo here

Ingredients:

Directions:

Fine Dining at Home

Recipe #: _____

Place photo here

Ingredients:

Directions:

Fine Dining at Home

Recipe #: _____

Place photo here

Ingredients:

Directions:

Fine Dining at Home

Recipe #: _____

Place photo here

Ingredients:

Directions:

Fine Dining at Home
Recipe #: _____

Place photo here

Ingredients:

Directions:

Fine Dining at Home

Recipe #: _____

Place photo here

Ingredients:

Directions:

Fine Dining at Home

Recipe #: _____

Place photo here

Ingredients:

Directions:

Fine Dining at Home

Recipe #: _____

Place photo here

Ingredients:

Directions:

Fine Dining at Home

Recipe #: _____

Place photo here

Ingredients:

Directions:

Fine Dining at Home
Recipe #: _____

Place photo here

Ingredients:

Directions:

Fine Dining at Home

Recipe #: _____

Place photo here

Ingredients:

Directions:

Fine Dining at Home

Recipe #: _____

Place photo here

Ingredients:

Directions:

Fine Dining at Home

Recipe #: _____

Place photo here

Ingredients:

Directions:

Fine Dining at Home

Recipe #: _____

Place photo here

Ingredients:

Directions:

Fine Dining at Home

Recipe #: _____

Place photo here

Ingredients:

Directions:

Fine Dining at Home

Recipe #: _____

Place photo here

Ingredients:

Directions:

Fine Dining at Home

Recipe #: _____

Place photo here

Ingredients:

Directions:

Fine Dining at Home
Recipe #: _____

Place photo here

Ingredients:

Directions:

www.ingramcontent.com/pod-product-compliance
Ingram Content Group UK Ltd.
Pitfield, Milton Keynes, MK11 3LW, UK
UKHW050414240426
12048UKWH00020B/1504